DARK METRO
VOLUME 1
TM
STORY BY TOKYO CALEN
ART BY YOSHIKEN

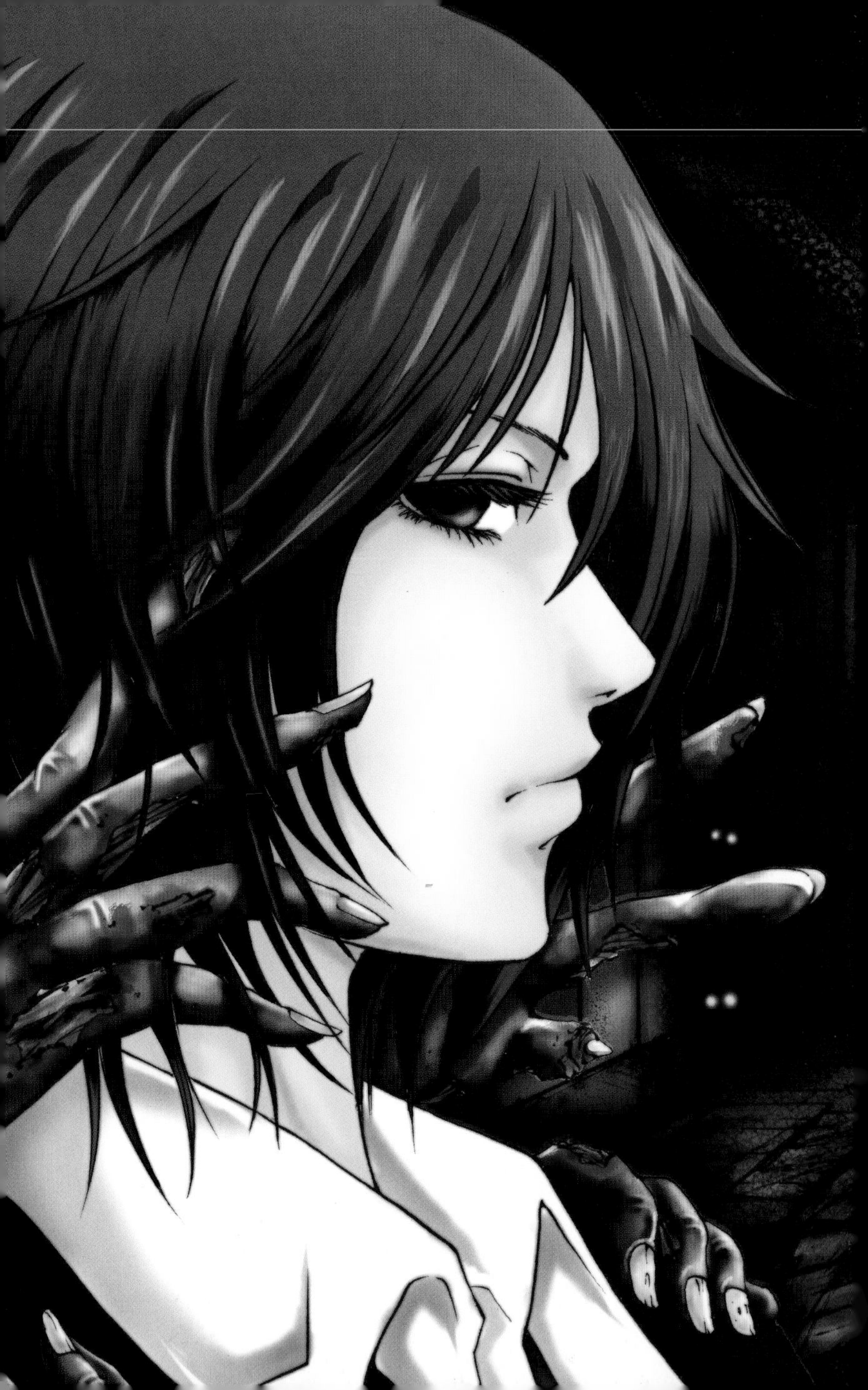

Table of Contents

Ikebukuro
Yurakucho L
Shinjuku
Oedo Line
Marunouchi Line
Meiji-jingumae
(Harajuku)
Chiyoda Line
Shibuya
Ginza Line

Stick around at the end of *Dark Metro* for a sneak peek into the gothic world of... (pg 172)

Doors of Chaos

DARK METRO

VOLUME 1

VOLUME 1

STORY BY TOKYO CALEN

ART BY YOSHIKEN

TOKYOPOP®

HAMBURG // LONDON // LOS ANGELES // TOKYO

Dark Metro Volume 1
Story by Tokyo Calen
Art by Yoshiken

Translation - Aska Yoshizu
English Adaptation - Kereth Cowe-Spigai
Retouch and Lettering - Star Print Brokers
Production Artist - Katherine Schilling
Graphic Designer - Colin Graham

Editor - Katherine Schilling
Digital Imaging Manager - Chris Buford
Pre-Production Supervisor - Erika Terriquez
Production Manager - Elisabeth Brizzi
Managing Editor - Vy Nguyen
Creative Director - Anne Marie Horne
Editor-in-Chief - Rob Tokar
Publisher - Mike Kiley
President and C.O.O. - John Parker
C.E.O. and Chief Creative Officer - Stuart Levy

A TOKYOPOP® Manga

TOKYOPOP Inc.
5900 Wilshire Blvd. Suite 2000
Los Angeles, CA 90036

E-mail: info@TOKYOPOP.com
Come visit us online at www.TOKYOPOP.com

ISBN: 978-1-4278-0740-3

First TOKYOPOP printing: February 2008
10 9 8 7 6 5 4 3 2 1
Printed in the USA

THEY GO THROUGH THEIR DAY TO DAY ROUTINE, NEVER SUSPECTING THAT IN THE SUBWAY TUNNELS...
...IS A GAP BETWEEN THE LAND OF THE LIVING AND THE LAND OF THE DEAD.

CHAPTER 1
GINZA STATION

1!
2!
3!
ACTING SCHOOL
STAY TOGETHER!
EYES UP! DON'T LOOK DOWN!!
ALL RIGHT. GOOD ENOUGH. LET'S CALL IT A DAY.
Yes, sir!
NICE WORK TODAY.
THANKS. YOU, TOO!
ANNA?
YES, TADOKORO-SENSEI?

AS THE LEAD IN THIS MUSICAL, IT'S *YOUR* JOB TO SET AN EXAMPLE FOR THE OTHERS.
SO, KEEP UP THE GOOD WORK!
THANK YOU, SENSEI, I WILL!
GOOD. HAVE A SAFE TRIP HOME.
YOU, TOO.
......
REI...
WHY HAVEN'T YOU BEEN COMING TO REHEARSALS...?
EVERYONE'S SAYING YOU MUST HAVE KILLED YOURSELF OVER YOUR AFFAIR WITH SENSEI.
OH, REI. THAT CAN'T BE TRUE, CAN IT?

Tokyo Metro
GINZA STATION
HUFF!
HUFF!
Attention, the last train will be leaving shortly.
OH, NO!!
WAIT. WAIT!!
Doors are now closing. Please watch your step.
NO WAY!!
.....

THAT WAS THE LAST TRAIN...
FANTASTIC.
IT'S A CAB FOR ME, I GUESS.
HUH?
WHAT THE--? THEY CLOSED THE DOORS ALREADY?!
NNGH!!
IMPOS-SIBLE. IT'S LOCKED...
THIS HAS NEVER HAPPENED BEFORE!

Sigh...
THERE'S NO ONE AROUND TO HELP. I GUESS I'M STUCK HERE UNTIL SOMEONE SHOWS UP.
......
SURE IS CREEPY DOWN HERE...
CLK
CLK
... WHAT'S THAT?
CLK
CLK
CLK
CLK
CLK
!

REI?!
ANNA! HELLO. LONG TIME NO SEE.
REI... WHAT ARE YOU DOING IN THE TUNNEL?
I MISSED THE LAST TRAIN SO I WALKED UP HERE ALONG THE TRACK, HOPING THIS STATION WAS STILL OPEN.
NO LUCK. THIS ONE'S CLOSED, TOO.
WOW, SHE LOOKS GREAT. SO MUCH FOR THE SUICIDE THEORY.
C'MON. WE CAN WALK UP TO THE NEXT STATION.
DON'T YOU THINK THAT STATION WILL BE CLOSED, TOO?

CAN'T HURT TO CHECK. COME ON!
MOVE IT, ANNA!
WE'RE WALKING, NOW!!
.....
I DON'T KNOW. IT'S AWFULLY DARK DOWN THERE.
DON'T WORRY, ANNA. I'LL LOOK AFTER YOU.
UM...
I THINK I'LL JUST STAY HERE.

WHAT WAS THAT NOISE?!
YOU'RE COMING WITH ME, ANNA...
...DOWN TO THE DARK WORLD!!
THE WHAT?
Dark world?
I'M TRAPPED DOWN HERE BECAUSE OF YOU! I WASN'T CAST AS LEAD AND IT WAS YOUR FAULT!
MY FAULT? SENSEI CHOSE ME. HOW COULD I CONTROL THAT?
OH, THAT'S IT. PLAY THE INNOCENT ONE!!
I LOVED HIM, ANNA. LOVED HIM!
I WORKED SO HARD, JUST TO PLEASE HIM. YOU HAVE NO IDEA HOW HARD I WORKED.
OH, GOD... REI?

AND STILL, HE CAST ME ASIDE AND CHOSE YOU.
YOU DON'T LOVE HIM THE WAY I DO!!
I WON'T HAVE IT!!
REI, NO...
I DIED BECAUSE OF YOU, YOU LITTLE SLUT!
REI, NO. YOU'RE NOT YOURSELF!!
ANNA...
DO YOU KNOW HOW IT FEELS...
...TO BE CRUSHED BY A TRAIN?
NO... NO...!

HOW DO YOU LIKE THAT?
MY LEG WAS CUT CLEAN OFF.
EEK!!
DON'T THINK I'LL BE DANCING ANYMORE, DO YOU?
OH GOD, OH GOD, OH GOD...
NOOOOOOOOOO!

HEH HEH...
A LITTLE SQUEAMISH?
AHA HA HA HA HA!
Huff!
Huff!
WHAT IN THE HELL IS GOING ON?!
Huff!
Huff!
WHAT WAS THAT?
WAS IT...
...REALLY...
SLIP

OW!!
UUGH...
AAA... NNNAA...
?!
ANNAA...
...AAA...
AAA... NNN... NAAA!!
YOU'RE COMING WITH MEEEE!

NOOO!
STAY AWAY FROM ME!!
HUFF!
HUFF!
RRRRING
HUFF!
HUFF!
...WHAT THE HELL?
RRRING
RRRRING
BLOCKED
HOW AM I GETTING RECEPTION DOWN HERE?

BZZT
Go...to...the exit...with ligh...t...
BZZT
?!
...?
WHAT WAS THAT ALL ABOUT?
ANN-AAAA...
YOU CAN'T LEAVE.
YOU'RE COMING TO THE DARK WORLD...
...WITH ME...

GET AWAY!!
OH, GOD! STAY AWAY!!
AAAH!
HUFF!
HUFF!
SOMEONE HELP ME.
出口
Exit
ANYONE! HELP ME!
RRING
NOW A TEXT MESSAGE?
HOW THE HELL AM I SUPPOSED TO READ A TEXT RIGHT NOW?!
!

Station Office
OKAY.
I HAVE TO FIND A WAY OUT...
OH... MAYBE I COULD...
...SEND A MESSAGE. WHO JUST TEXTED ME?
No Signal
Go toward the exit with light.
THE EXIT WITH LIGHT?
AGAIN?!
THERE'S NO SIGNAL...BUT I'M GETTING MESSAGES!!
BBZT
BBZT
You can't get connected to the outside...
BBZT
EEEEK!!
Hurry to the exit with light.
WHAT EXIT WITH LIGHT?!
!!

HISS...

PLEASE...
...DON'T NOTICE ME...
PLIP
PLOP
.....
HUFF...
HUFF...
Get up! Get out of there!!
HOW?! I'M TRAPPED! I CAN'T GET OUT!
BZZT
You can't hide here much longer.
BZZT
EH?

OH, GOD!
AAAAAAAH!

WHEEZE...
HUFF...
"HURRY TO THE EXIT WITH LIGHT."
.....
HUFF!
HUFF!
THE EXIT WITH LIGHT...?
WHAT THE HECK IS HE TALKING ABOUT?!
出口 Exit A9
OH!!

AN EXIT!
AN EXIT WITH LIGHT...!
PLEASE !!
HELP !!
OPEN UP!!
SOME- BODY!!!
HELP... ME...
THERE IS...
...NO WAY OUT...

ANNA, I WANT YOU TO DIE, LIKE ME...
REI?!
RAAAWRR!
AANNNNAAA!
NO!!
NOOOOO!!
AAAAH!

WHERE COULD IT BE?!
AN EXIT WITH LIGHT...?!
!!
THAT'S IT! IT'S ALL OVER!!!
BE SILENT.

?!
AA
ANNNA!
!!
COME...
...WITH ME...
ANNAAAAAAAAAA...
OKAY, I THINK SHE'S GONE...
.....

WAS THAT YOU?
ON THE PHONE?
.....
LISTEN TO ME. WHEN THE CAMERA GOES OFF...
...JUMP INTO THE LIGHT OF THE FLASH.
?!
JUMP INTO THE LIGHT?!
ARE YOU CRAZY?!
YOU SHOULDN'T BE HERE...
THE UNDERWORLD IS NOT FOR YOU YET.
?
THE FLAME OF YOUR LIFE BURNS BRIGHTLY STILL.

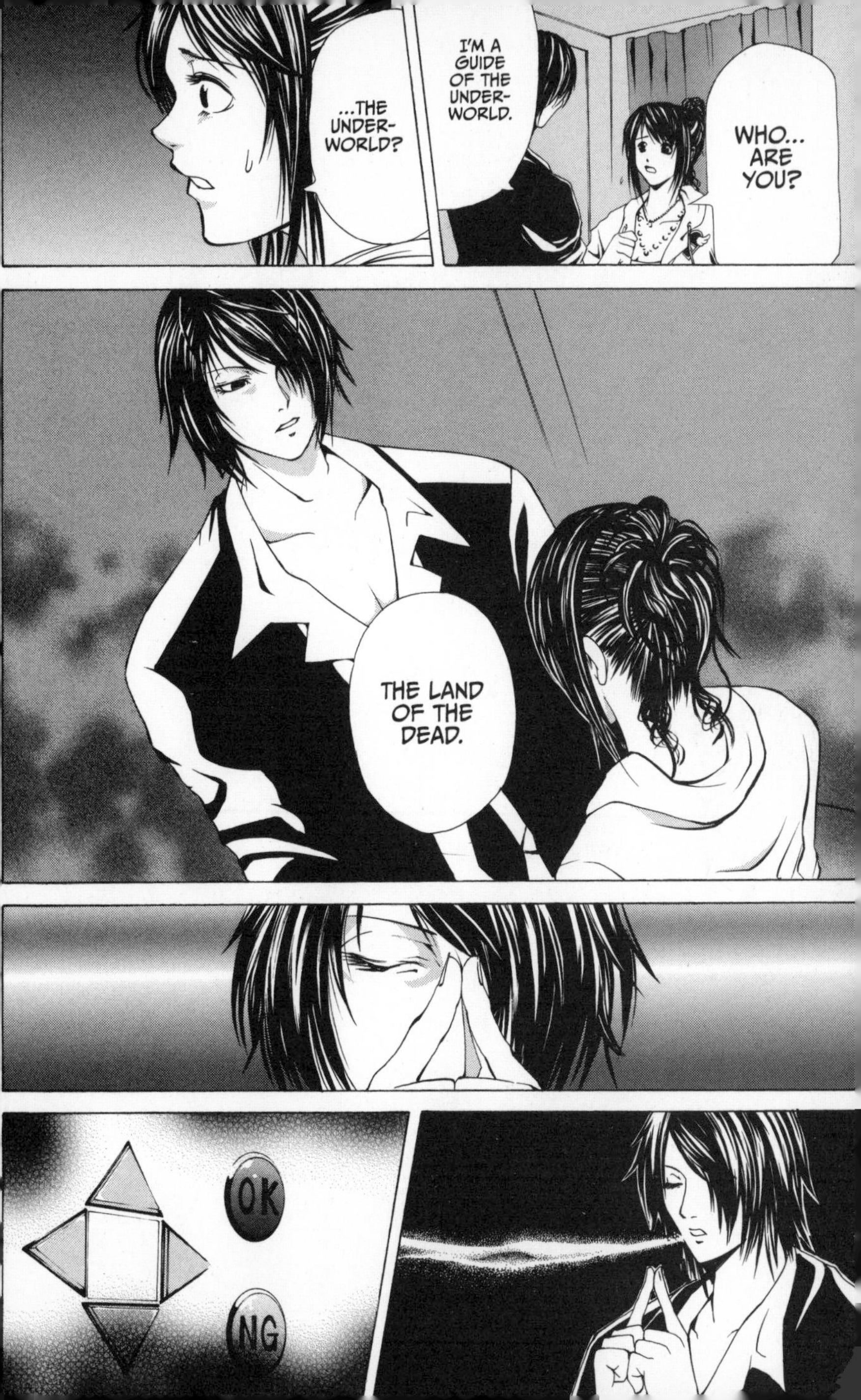
WHO... ARE YOU?
I'M A GUIDE OF THE UNDER-WORLD.
...THE UNDER-WORLD?
THE LAND OF THE DEAD.
OK
NG

VVMMMM
?!
KOFF
WHAT'S GOING ON? THE CAMERA IS ON?
BUT WHY...?
LOOK STRAIGHT INTO THE LENS AND ALIGN YOUR CHIN WITH THE BOTTOM LINE.
DON'T MISS THE FLASH, ANNA.
WHAT? I DON'T UNDER-STAND...
?!
WAIT! WHAT'S YOUR NAME?!
.....

I AM CALLED... SEIYA.
WAIT!
DON'T...
...LEAVE...
...ME!
SEIYA?!
WHERE ARE YOU?!
PLEASE! DON'T LEAVE ME ALONE!
PLEASE...
?!

HA
HA
HA...
HA
HA
HA!!
HA
HA!
NO MORE
HIDING!
AAAAH!
UNGH!

ANN...
...NAA...
...AAA...
SHOOTING IN... ...3...2...
CAN'T... BREATH.
1.

GYAAAAAH!
!!
THE EXIT...
...WITH LIGHT?!

AAA
AAAAH!

!!
HUFF!
HUFF!
A...
...DREAM?
.....
MORE LIKE A NIGHTMARE.

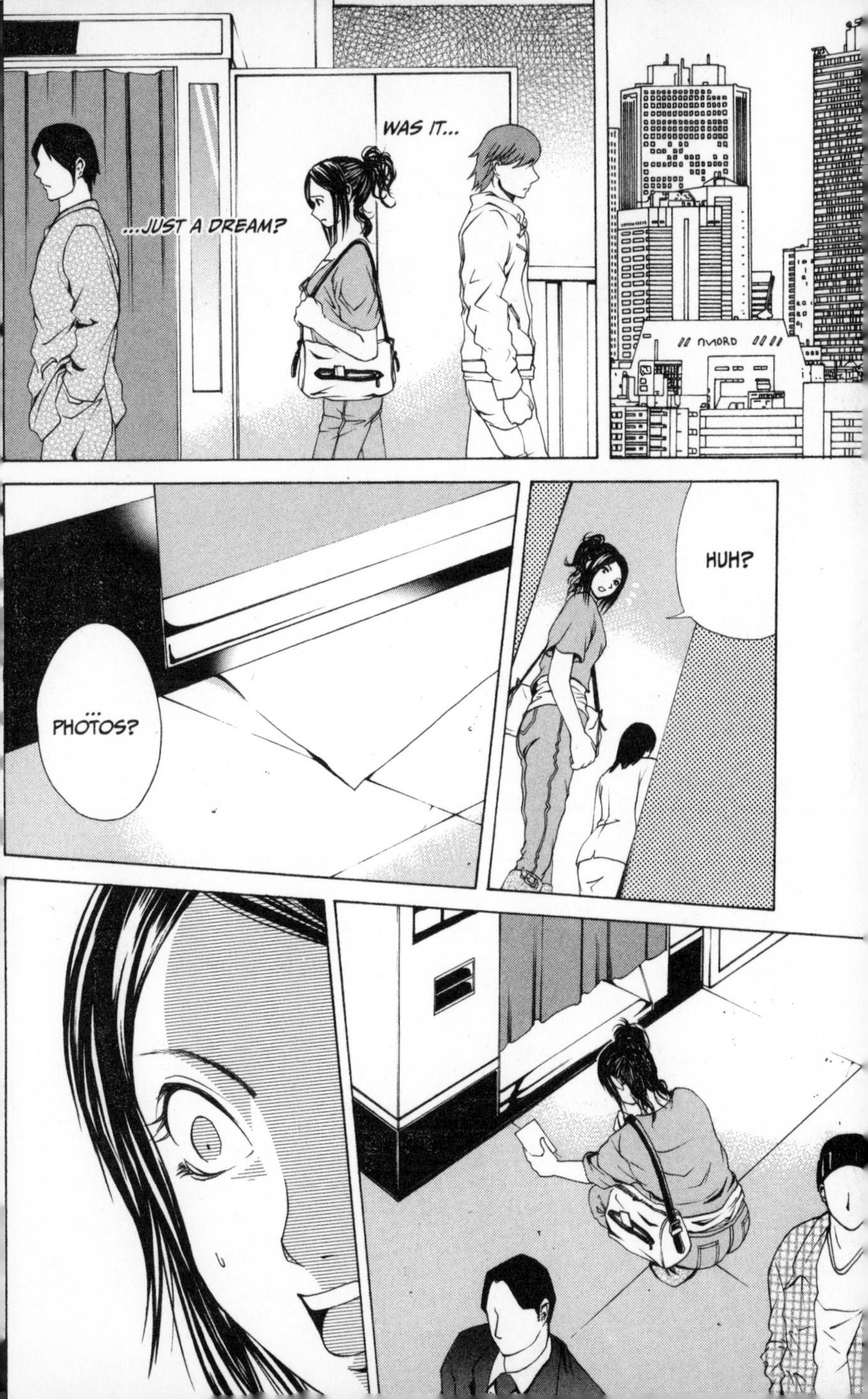
WAS IT...
...JUST A DREAM?
HUH?
...PHOTOS?

THESE ARE...
...FROM LAST NIGHT.
IT REALLY...
...HAPPENED...
.....

EVER SINCE THAT NIGHT...
...WHEN I'M IN THE SUBWAY...
...I LOOK FOR HIM. SEYIA. THE ONE WHO SAVED MY LIFE...

CHAPTER 11
SHIBUYA STATION

High School Girl Brutally Murdered

SHEESH.
WHAT A DRAG.
PARENTS CAN BE SUCH A PAIN.
NOBORU! HOW DARE YOU THROW AWAY YOUR SCHOOL WORK?!
AND WHAT IS THIS SCORE?!
.....

SIGH... I'D RATHER BE ANYWHERE BUT SCHOOL TODAY.
HEY, GIRL, YOU WANNA KARAOKE WITH ME?
YOU'RE TOO CUTE FOR THIS PLACE. YOU AND ME SHOULD HOOK UP.
SCAMMING. DO GIRLS REALLY FALL FOR THAT CRAP?
MAYBE THEY DO. IT'S NOT LIKE I KNOW HOW TO GET A GIRL.
Sigh...
?!
HUH?
MM?
HEY, NOBORU!
NOBORU?
TERUO, HEY. AND SHOUTA.

WHAT ARE YOU GUYS UP TO?
SAME AS YOU. SKIPPING SCHOOL.
SO, YOU GUYS ARE TRYING TO PICK UP GIRLS?
IT MAY LOOK THAT WAY, BUT WE'RE MORE FOR MAKING CASH.
WANT IN ON THE ACTION, NOBORU?
?
WHAAAAAT?!
YOU MEAN LIKE AN ESCORT SERVICE?!
HEY, MAN, KEEP IT DOWN.

ARE YOU THOSE GUYS WHO INTRODUCE GIRLS TO OLDER MEN?
WE JUST KNOW SOME OLD GUYS THAT WANT COMPANY, SO WE FIND GIRLS TO INTRODUCE THEM TO.
AND WE GET A LITTLE CASH FOR OUR TROUBLES.
THEY'RE PIMPING!
WE HAVEN'T HAD MUCH LUCK TODAY.
MAYBE WE SHOULD TRY ANOTHER SPOT.
HEY!

YEP.
WOW, SHE'S CUTE!
.....
DO YOU THINK YOU COULD INTRODUCE ME TO SOMEONE?
I DON'T THINK YOU'RE THE RIGHT TYPE OF GIRL.
Sigh...
TERUO?!
I THINK SHE'S A LITTLE, ER... CONSERVATIVE, DON'T YOU?
ARE YOU KIDDING? C'MON, SHE'S BEAUTIFUL!
WHAT? YOU DON'T WANT ME?
WELL, I HAVE LOTS OF FRIENDS WHO ARE INTERESTED, TOO.
.....
SEE? JACKPOT!
FOR REAL...?

WHERE ARE...
...YOUR FRIENDS?
WELL, TONIGHT...
...ALL OF US ARE GOING TO THIS CLUB.
NOBORU, WHAT DID YOU TELL YOUR PARENTS?
YEAH, AREN'T THEY KINDA STRICT?
THEY THINK I'M STUDYING AT TERUO'S HOUSE.

STUDYING?! THAT'S A GOOD ONE.
PARENTS ARE SUCKERS.
YOU EVER HEARD OF A CLUB DOWN HERE?
NOPE.
MUST BE A SECRET.
I DON'T THINK THERE IS ONE.
RIGHT.
BRRRRING
HUH?
OH, A TEXT...
BRRRRING
vvvmmm
"LEAVE?"
Leave.
WHAT IS THIS? SOME KIND OF JOKE?
HI, GUYS!
!
YOU'RE ALL HERE?
WHY'S SHE WEARING HER UNIFORM TO A CLUB?

SO, WHERE'S THIS CLUB?
WE'VE NEVER HEARD OF ONE DOWN HERE.
HEE HEE...
HERE.
Storage Box
HUH? ARE YOU MESSING WITH US?
Tee-hee!
STAIRS...UNDER THE BOX?!

DAMN.
NO WAY!
IT'S DOWN HERE.
IT'S LIKE A MOVIE.
BRRRRING
BLOCKED. I WONDER WHO...?
BRRRRING
Receiving call from blocked number.
BEEP
Do not follow !!
?!
HUH?
It is dangerous down there!!
WHAT IS HE...?
WRONG NUMBER?
NOBORU, HURRY UP!
I'M COMING.

WOW...
OVER HERE, GUYS!!
WE'RE MARI'S FRIENDS.
A PLEASURE TO MEET YOU.

HEY!
WAIT UP--
BLOCKED NUMBER? AGAIN?!
VVVVMM
BRRR RING
Get out of there as fast as you can. You shouldn't be there.
WHAT DO YOU WANT?! CUT IT OUT!
I DON'T KNOW WHAT YOU'RE TALKING ABOUT. STOP CALLING!
IS THAT TRUE?
HA HA HA!
DAMN THEM...
VVVVVMM
YOU DON'T KNOW WHEN TO QUIT...
BRRRRING
ACK!!
Receiving call from
▸ Mom
SHIT, I CAN'T ANSWER DOWN HERE. IT'S TOO LOUD. SHE'LL KNOW I'M NOT AT TERUO'S STUDYING.
WHAT DO YOU WANT? WE JUST GOT STARTED WITH OUR STUDYING...

WHO...
...IS THIS GUY?
......
ガッ
?!
ぐい

H-HEY!
WHAT DO YOU THINK YOU'RE DOING?!
OOPH!
WHAT'S YOUR PROB-LEM?!
.....
JUST SHUT UP AND LEAVE.
HUH? WHO THE HELL DO YOU THINK YOU ARE?!
BESIDES, TERUO AND SHOUTA ARE STILL--

?!
THE ENTRANCE... IS GONE?!
THEY WON'T BE COMING BACK.
HEY, WAIT A MINUTE!
WHO ARE YOU...?
?!
.....
I'M A GUIDE TO THE UNDER-WORLD...

HE'S GONE?
OH... NO...
NOOOO!
S-SOMEBODY HELP!
TERUOOO!! SHOUTAAA!!!
CAN YOU HEAR ME?!
GET OUT OF THERE. GET OUT!!
CAN YOU HEAR ME? OH, GOD. WHAT HAPPENED TO THE ENTRANCE?! IT WAS JUST THERE!!
HEY!

WAAAAAAAAH!

HEY, EVERY-BODY!
IT'S TIME TO START THE *MAIN EVENT!*
WONDER WHAT IT'S GOING TO BE.
YEAH.
TODAY'S SPECIAL GUEST IS...
...*YOU!!*

ME?
?!
GYAAAAAAA!
TERUO!
GG

HOLY SHIT!
TERUO!!
NNFF...
TERUO ...!!

......
AAA
AAAAAAH!

OH NO, NO, NO! TERUO...
BLRMPH!
TERUO...
UGH...
GIVE IT UP FOR A STUNNING PERFORMANCE FROM OUR SPECIAL GUEST!
WASN'T IT GREAT?
!!
NOW, SHALL WE MOVE ONTO THE SECOND STAGE?
HUH?

NOW IT'S *YOUR* TURN.
WAAAAH!
C'MON!
OPEN UP!!
!!

AAH!
W-WHAT ARE YOU?!
WHY ARE YOU DOING THIS TO US?
I'M DEAD. BECAUSE OF YOU.
...?!
TO KEEP MY FRIEND FROM MEETING THAT JOHN YOU SET HER UP WITH...
...I WENT IN HER PLACE TO TELL THE MAN TO FORGET ABOUT IT. HE *MURDERED* ME!

THE MAN THAT YOU'VE BEEN INTRODUCING TO GIRLS...
DID YOU KNOW THAT HE'S A MURDERER?!
THAT... THAT ISN'T MY FAULT...
SO YOU SAY. BUT NOW YOU'LL SEE WHAT IT'S LIKE TO DIE LIKE THAT.
NOOO!
AAAH!
CRUNCH
UGHH!
SNAP
THUD
AAHH...!
THUD
SNAP

PLEASE
...
AAH...
AAAH!
NO...
AAAH!
UNGH!
OW...
!
...?
MY... ROOM?
HUH?
HOW DID I END UP HERE?
I THOUGHT I MET TERUO AND SHOUTA AND...
HUH...

MM... I CAN'T REMEMBER. WHERE DID WE GO?
DRAT. NEITHER OF THEM ARE ANSWER-ING.
カッ
カッ
MESSAGE BOARD
Teruo and Shouta,
Hey, guys. Call me.
-Noboru

……
スウウ

CHAPTER III
IKEBUKURO STATION

EXCUSE ME.
!
HI, I'M THE NEW TRAIN OPERATOR FOR IKEBUKURO STATION.
THIS IS MY FIRST DAY.
AOSHIMA-KUN, NICE TO MEET YOU!
IT'S NICE TO MEET YOU, TOO!
I'M SERIOUS!
I CAN SEE THAT, BUT NONE OF THE OTHER PASSENGERS SAW ANYTHING.
?

BUT IT HAPPENED!
?!
YOU HAVE TO BELIEVE ME!
I WAS STANDING BY THE DOOR WHEN...
ゴトン
ゴトン
ゴオオオ

KI...
KILL... ME...
...!
UWAAAAAAAH!

THERE HAD TO BE SOMEONE ON THE ROOF OF THAT TRAIN!
I'M SORRY. IT'S JUST HARD TO BELIEVE THAT SOMEONE WAS ON THE ROOF OF A RUNNING TRAIN.
EXCUSE ME, SIR. HAVE YOU BEEN DRINKING TODAY?
HEY. DON'T TOUCH ME!
WAIT A SECOND! YOU HAVE TO LISTEN--
.....
WE GET NUT JOBS LIKE THAT FROM TIME TO TIME. IT'S BEST TO JUST IGNORE THEM.
ERR... OKAY.
.....
AOSHIMA, ARE YOU GETTING SPOOKED BY THE RUMOR THAT GOES AROUND THE TRAINING CLASSES?
YIPE!

WHAT'S... THE RUMOR?
DON'T YOU KNOW?
WOOOH
THEY SAY THE SUBWAY...
...IS HAUNTED.
.....
THEY SAY THAT THERE ARE PASSAGES TO THE UNDERWORLD IN THE TUNNELS...
...AND THAT THE DEAD WANDER THE SUBWAY.
.....
?

HA HA HA!
SENPAI, YOU DON'T REALLY BELIEVE THAT, DO YOU? IS THIS A FIRST-DAY PRANK?
I DON'T BELIEVE IN THAT STUFF, SO IF YOU'RE TRYING TO SPOOK ME, IT WON'T WORK!
YOU'RE NO FUN.
ゴオォ
MARUNOUCHI-SEN: BETWEEN KOURAKUEN STATION AND MYOUGADANI STATION.
THE SETTING SUN IS TOO BRIGHT.
THE SUBWAY IS ABOVE GROUND ONCE...
...AFTER PASSING MYOUGADANI STATION...
ガタン
ガタン

...AND THEN IT'S DARKNESS.
オオォ...
IT'S CREEPY AS HELL DOWN HERE...
NO WONDER PEOPLE SAY IT'S HAUNTED.

ブォオオ
Ikebukuro
BILLS
THE LAST STATION'S JUST AFTER THIS TURN.
MY FIRST SHIFT WAS NICE AND SMOOTH.

Ikebukuro
?!

WHERE ...?
I COULD HAVE SWORN...
I MUST BE GETTING TIRED! GET A GRIP!!
Last stop, Ikebukuro Station
HUH...?

WHEW...
HEY, YOU MADE IT!
WHAT'S WRONG? YOU DON'T LOOK SO GOOD.
NOTHING... I'M FINE.
DAMMIT, FIRST DAY AND IT'S ALREADY GETTING TO ME.
THERE'S NO WAY THAT SOMEBODY WAS SITTING IN THE TUNNEL.
GOOD MORNING.
HUH?
MURMUR
MURMUR
SENPAI, DID SOMETHING HAPPEN?
OH, AOSHIMA. YES. IN FACT...

...ANOTHER DRIVER WAS HOSPITALIZED.
IT'S YOUR FIRST DAY, SO YOU COULDN'T BE EXPECTED TO KNOW.
REALLY? HOW... COME?
HE WITNESSED A TRAIN JUMPER.
WHAT?!

WHEN YOU'RE DRIVING A TRAIN, YOUR HEADLIGHTS ARE BRIGHT, YA KNOW?
SO, WHEN SOMEONE JUMPS IN FRONT OF A TRAIN, IT SEEMS TO HAPPEN IN SLOW MOTION.
SOMETIMES, THE DRIVER IS CLOSE ENOUGH TO LOOK THE JUMPER IN THE EYE. IT'S REALLY QUITE TRAUMATIC. MOST DRIVERS DON'T COME BACK FROM THAT.
IN THIS CASE, THERE WAS NO BODY.
?!
W-WHAT HAPPENED TO IT?!
PEOPLE ARE SAYING IT MUST HAVE BEEN THE GHOST...
...OF A SUICIDE WHO'S TRYING TO KILL HIMSELF OVER AND OVER.
......

C-COME ON!
ARE YOU TRYING TO SPOOK ME AGAIN?
.....
WHO COULD DO THIS JOB IF HE BELIEVED GHOSTS WANDERED THE TRACKS?
BUT...
GIVE THE GHOST ANGLE A REST. I'LL GO AND TAKE OVER HIS DRIVING SHIFT!
.....

GHOSTS? THEY'RE ALL OUT OF THEIR MINDS!
.....
PFFT! STUPID.
Thank you for using Tokyo Metro Marunouchi-sen today.
ガタン
This train is bound for Ikebukuro Station.
I DON'T BELIEVE ANY OF IT.
EVERY-BODY IS OVER-REACTING!
MAYBE I WAS TELLING MYSELF THAT BECAUSE I NEEDED TO BELIEVE THERE WERE NO GHOSTS.

.....
THIS TIME, I WELCOMED THE BRIGHT SUN.
GOOD... IT'S ALMOST THE LAST STATION...
Ikebukuro

PLEASE...
...KILL... ME...
SOMEONE ON THE TRACK?!
HooooooNK

SHIT! HE'S REALLY THERE!
THE BRAKE--!
?!

Ikebukuro
STOP, DAMMIT!
THE BRAKE...
...ISN'T WORKING?!
STOP!!

WAAAA
AAAAA
A!

NOOOOOO!

AH...
ガタ
ガタ
NO...
I...
I DID IT...
I JUST...
オオオオ...
JUST KILLED A--!!
!
AAH...
AAAH...

OH GOD!!!
NO NO NO!
KILL...
...MEE EEE...
AAAAAH!

PLEASE... FORGIVE ME... I...
THE BRAKE... IT DIDN'T-- IT WAS THE BRAKE...

AOSHIMA...
I KNOW YOU SAID YOU USED THE EMERGENCY BRAKE AND THE HORN, BUT THE CONTROL ROOM REPORTS THAT YOU DIDN'T ACTIVATE EITHER.
BESIDES...
WHEN WE WENT TO RECOVER THE BODY, NOTHING WAS THERE, NOT EVEN A SINGLE DROP OF BLOOD.
NO... THAT CAN'T BE...
I DID... I DID... HIT A...
I THINK YOU NEED SOME TIME OFF.
WHY...? I KNOW...
I KNOW WHAT I SAW.
AND I FELT THE IMPACT...

BRRRRING
A TEXT?
FROM WHO?
KSSSH
KSSHT
KI...LL
ME...
KSSHT
?!
PLE...
EEASE...
KI...LL
ME...

KILL ME!!
GYAAAAAAH!
NNGH...
HHNK...

YOU'VE BEEN DEAD FOR A LONG TIME NOW.
I WANT TO DIE ALREADY...
WHY... CAN'T I...?
IF I'M REALLY DEAD...
...THEN, WHY AM I STILL SUFFER-ING?
YOU KILLED YOURSELF TO ESCAPE YOUR PAIN...
SHRIEK!
...AND AS ONE WHO ONLY SEEKS AN ESCAPE...
...YOU WILL NEVER FIND IT, EVEN IN DEATH.

THE OTHER DAY, ANOTHER TRAIN OPERATOR WAS HOSPITALIZED.
ANOTHER ONE... WHY?
HE SAW SOMETHING ON THE TRACK.
.....
A ghost?
YEP. IT WAS HIS FIRST DAY. JUST LIKE YOU.
OH, COME ON. GIVE IT A REST.
I...saw...I did...
MUMBLING
MUMBLING
...hit him... I...

CHAPTER IV
SHINJUKU STATION

すずき
COFFEE
KABUKICHO ICHIBANGAI
1F
DUNE
WE JUST GOT AN ORDER FOR A BOTTLE OF DOM PÉRIGNON AT TABLE THREE!
THREE CHEERS, EVERYONE!
HEY, YOU KNOW NATSUKO-SAN HASN'T BEEN AROUND LATELY.
SHE WAS BIG ON THE DOM PÉRIGNON, TOO, WASN'T SHE?
...!
YOU SEEN HER AROUND, JIN-SAN?
I DON'T KNOW WHERE SHE IS...
MAYBE SHE WENT HOME TO VISIT OR SOME-THING.
"NATSUKO-SAN! SAY CHEESE!"

JIN-CHAN, YOU HAVE TO GIVE ME ONE OF THOSE PICTURES.
YEAH, OF COURSE.
A BOTTLE OF DOM TODAY, NATSUKO-SAN?
.....
OH, UM... NO. I DON'T FEEL LIKE IT TODAY.
!
UH... OKAY.

LEAVE ME ALONE, NATSUKO. WE'RE DONE.
JIN-CHAN... I JUST WANTED...
ENOUGH...
YOU TOLD ME YOU'RE A BIG CEO. LIAR.
YOU'RE ALL ALIKE.
YOU'RE DROWNING IN DEBT, BUT STILL COME INTO THE BAR AND THROW YOUR MONEY AROUND.
I ONLY DID IT FOR YOU, JIN-CHAN.
TOUGH SHIT. WHEN YOU'RE OUT OF MONEY, THAT'S THE END.

NO! I CAN'T BELIEVE THAT!
DON'T TOUCH ME!
AAAH!
IRRI-TATING BITCH...
koff
koff
UGH...
JIN... CHAN... JIN-CHAN...
WHAT DO YOU WANT?

JIN-CHAN...
LET'S DIE... TOGETHER...
W-WAIT. NATSUKO ...?
YOU CAN'T BE...
PUT THAT DOWN!
JIN-CHAN...
WHOA!
AAH!
THWUNK

PANT...
PANT...
PANT...
PANT...

ズル
SHIT...
SHE'S HEAVY...
ズル
ゴポ
ゴポ
IT'S YOUR OWN FAULT...
...NATSUKO-SAN.
YOUR FAULT...

EARTH TO JIN-SAN!
!
YOU'RE UP, PAL. TABLE THREE.
OH... RIGHT.
THANK YOU FOR WAITING.
"I DON'T KNOW," HE SAYS. THE GUY'S HEARTLESS.
HE'D BE NOTHING HERE IF IT WEREN'T FOR HER.
パァァ
18:20
AT THIS TIME OF DAY, SHINJUKU STATION IS PACKED WITH ESCORTS HEADING TO WORK.

I KNEW HE'D BE ON THIS TRAIN...
WHAT ARE YOU GOING TO DO? HE ISN'T DEAD YET.
I KNOW.
THIS FLAME OF LIFE...
スッ
I WILL PUT IT OUT.

ANOTHER DAY OF WORK.
!
HUH?
DUNE
HEY! HOW'S IT GOING?
NOT BAD.
HUH? WEREN'T YOU JUST WITH NATSUKO-SAN?

WHAT?
I SAW YOU WITH HER AT THE STATION, SO I THOUGHT SHE'D COME IN WITH YOU.
.....
NO...
NO WAY...
DAMN RYU. WHAT THE HELL WAS HE TALKING ABOUT?
HE SURE KNOWS HOW TO RUIN A GUY'S DAY.

WAS THAT ...?!
NATSU-KO?!
WAS THAT NATSU-KO?!
UUURGH!
WATCH IT!
MOVE IT!
OUT OF MY WAY!
PANT!
PANT!
SHIT... SHE'S GONE...

NATSU-KO...
KABUKICHO ICHIBANGAI
COULD SHE...
...SOMEHOW BE ALIVE?!
.....
SORRY, MIND IF I CUT IN?
YOU OKAY?
.....
!

WHAT'S GOING ON, JIN-SAN? YOU'VE BEEN ACTING WEIRD LATELY.
IT'S NOTHING. LEAVE ME ALONE.
BRRRING
A TEXT...?
...!
▶ Sender: Natsuko
I will never forgive you for stabbing me.
I will never forgive you for what you've done.
.....

SHIT!
UGH!
WHAT THE HELL IS WRONG WITH YOU? ARE TRYING TO PUT THIS BAR OUT OF BUSINESS?!
YOUR SALES ARE IN THE TOILET!
GET YOUR HEAD ON STRAIGHT, OR YOU'RE FIRED!
.....

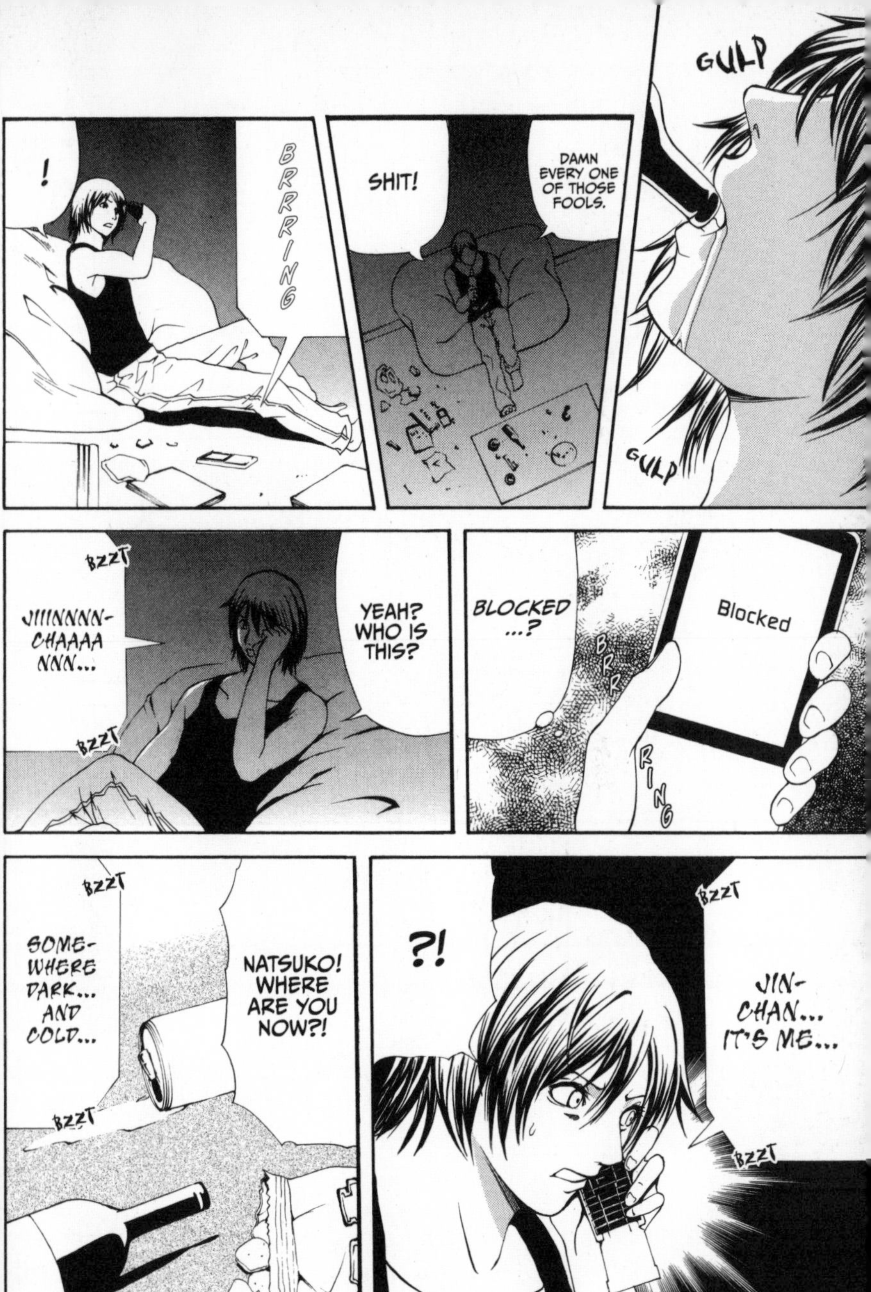
GULP
GULP
DAMN EVERY ONE OF THOSE FOOLS.
SHIT!
BRRRING
!
Blocked
BLOCKED ...?
BRR
RING
YEAH? WHO IS THIS?
BZZT
JIIINNNN-CHAAAA NNN...
BZZT
BZZT
JIN-CHAN... IT'S ME...
?!
BZZT
NATSUKO! WHERE ARE YOU NOW?!
BZZT
SOME-WHERE DARK... AND COLD...
BZZT

KSSH
THIS TIME...
HEH... HEH.
NATSUKO...
...I'LL KILL YOU FOR GOOD!
ガチャ
ODAYOU
地下鉄
K's Art

Subnade 2
THAT BITCH! I AM GOING TO KILL HER. KILL HER FOR GOOD!!
THIS TIME, SHE'S DEAD!!!
HUH...?
IS THAT...
...NATSUKO?!

NATSUKO!!
STOP!
?!
WHOA!
HUFF!
HUFF!
?!

WHERE THE HELL DID SHE GO?!
!
I CAN'T LET HER GET AWAY!
SHE'S DEAD MEAT!
NATSUKO!
?!
DON'T TRY TO RUN FROM ME!

YOU'RE GONNA DIE!!
?!
SHIT. WHERE DID SHE GO?!
HEY.
COME OUT OF THERE!
BEEP
CRASH
H-HELLO, POLICE?
THERE'S A PSYCHO RUNNING AROUND WITH A KNIFE!
NATSUKO!!
YOU'RE DEAD!!

NA--
!
HEE HEE.
ARE YOU LAUGHING AT ME?!
I'LL KILL YOU, BITCH!
!
EEK!
LOOK OUT! HE'S GOT A KNIFE!

RUN!
WAAAH!
AAAAH!
NATSUKO!
WHERE DID YOU GO?!
JIN-CHAN.

HERE I AM, LOVE.

RAAAAA
WRR!

SLASH
SLASH
HACK

GYAAAAAH!
WAAAH!
CALL AN AMBULANCE!
I'M ON IT!
EEEEEK!
HOLY SHIT!
?!
WHAT'S GOING ON?
!

JIN... SAN?!
......
WHA--

WHAT THE HELL... IS... THIS...?
......
スッ
SUICIDE...
HOW DREAD-FUL!
JEEZ... LOOK AT ALL THAT BLOOD.

CHAPTER V
MEIJI-JINGUMAE STATION

WAKANA, WHAT ARE YOU READING?
OH, YOU KNOW...
THAT NEW "TRUE HORROR" BULLETIN BOARD.
"MIDNIGHT SUBWAY?"
IT'S A NEW POST...
I had missed the last train, and got locked in the station. This girl that I thought had committed suicide came out of the tunnel and attacked me.
I got away from her and was trying to find the way out. I thought she would find me and kill me for sure when...

...suddenly a man showed up and told me to jump into the flash of the photo booth. I thought he was just nuts, but it worked. I escaped.
After introducing himself as Seiya, he just disappeared. Ever since that night, I've been looking for him in the subway.
...SEIYA?
HEY WAKANA, LET'S GO.
OKAY.
SEIYA... THAT NAME SOUNDS FAMILIAR...
?
WHERE HAVE I HEARD IT BEFORE?
SEIYA...

WH-
WHOA!
OOSH
GAWD, WHERE DID THAT WIND COME FROM SO SUDDENLY?!
DAMN. MY HAIR IS TRASHED.
HA HA HA...
HUH?
HEY, HOW DID YOU GET THAT SCAR?
OH, THIS?
I WAS IN AN ACCIDENT WHEN I WAS LITTLE.
BACK THEN...
MY NAME IS WAKA-CHAN.

WHAT'S YOUR NAME, MISTER?
SEIYA.
MY NAME IS SEIYA.
THAT'S IT... THAT NAME!
WAKANA? YOU LOOK LIKE YOU SAW A GHOST.
UH...I HAVE TO GO. SORRY...
HUH? HEY, WAKANA?!

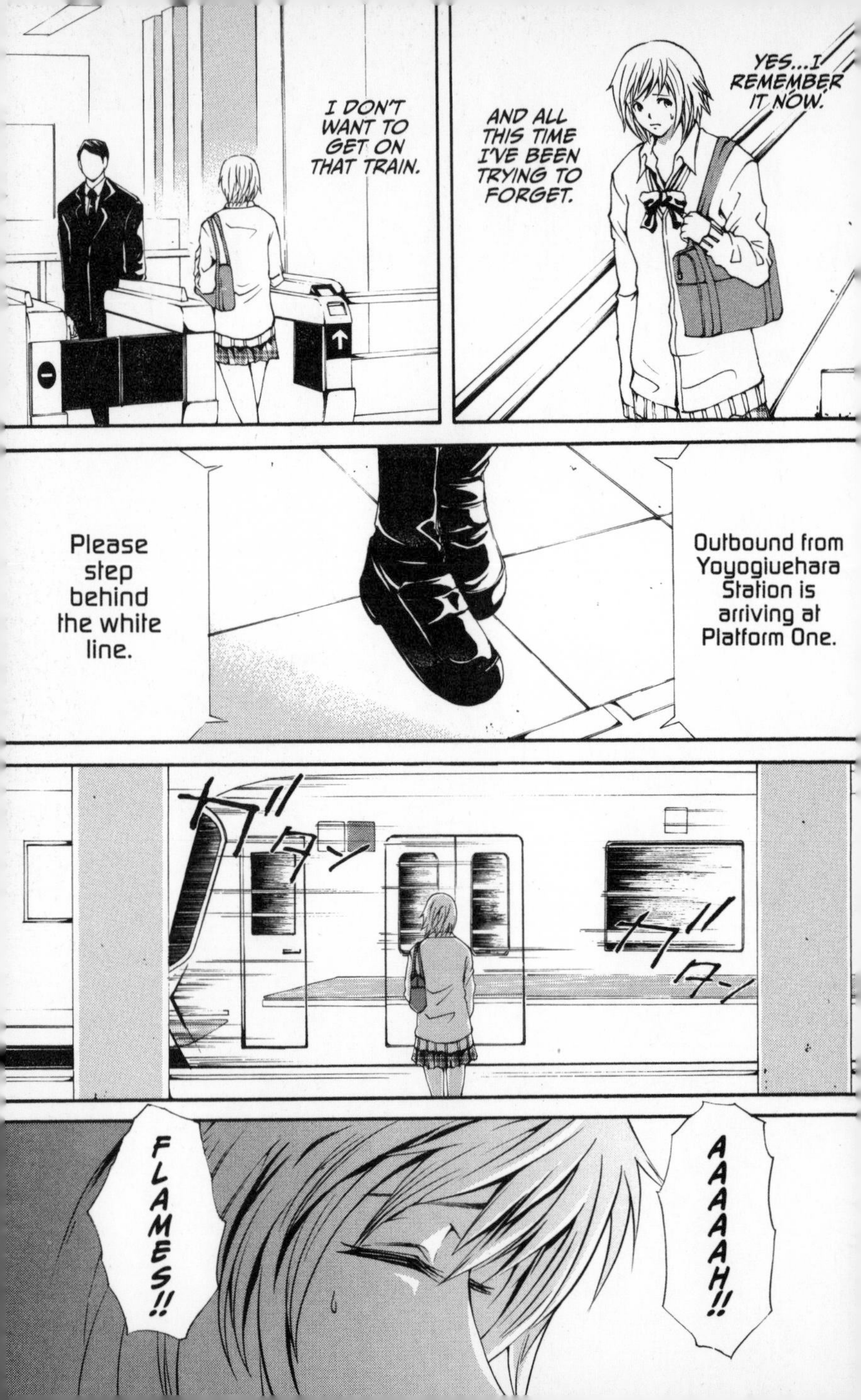
YES...I REMEMBER IT NOW.
AND ALL THIS TIME I'VE BEEN TRYING TO FORGET.
I DON'T WANT TO GET ON THAT TRAIN.
Outbound from Yoyogiuehara Station is arriving at Platform One.
Please step behind the white line.
ガタン
ガタン
AAAAAAH!!
FLAMES!!

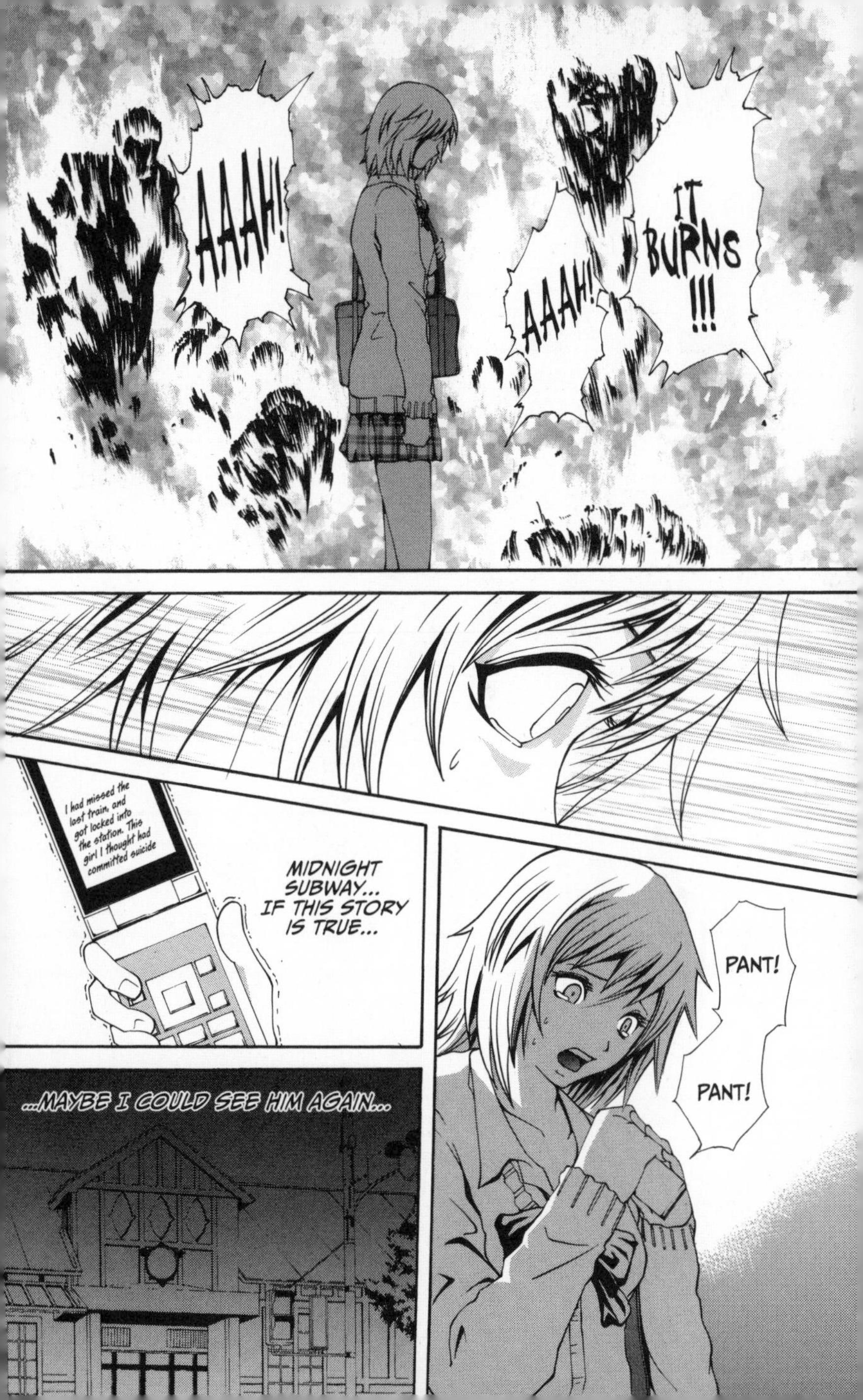
IT BURNS!!!
AAAH!
AAAH!
PANT!
PANT!
I had missed the last train, and got locked into the station. This girl I thought had committed suicide
MIDNIGHT SUBWAY... IF THIS STORY IS TRUE...
...MAYBE I COULD SEE HIM AGAIN...

ATM
TWO O'CLOCK...
IT SHOULD BE TIME...
HELLO? ANYONE THERE?
SEIYA-SAN...
I WANT TO SEE YOU AGAIN...

IT'S PITCH DARK HERE. AND CREEPY!
I WONDER IF SEIYA COULD REALLY BE HERE.
SEIYA-SAN.
IF YOU'RE HERE, PLEASE COME OUT.
WHOA! WHAT WAS THAT?!
YIPE!
HE'S NOT HERE.
WAS THE STORY MADE UP?

I GOT SO ANXIOUS TO FIND HIM.
SEIYA-SAN...
I FEEL SO STUPID...
オオ・・オ

HUH?!
WHY IS THERE A TRAIN?!
ガタン
プシュー
...?
I HAD NO IDEA THE TRAINS RAN THIS LATE.
AND IT'S SO FULL.

SEIYA-SAN...
I WANTED TO FIND HIM!
OH, WELL... I GUESS I'LL JUST HEAD HOME.
SEIYA-SAN...
For time adjustment, this train will stay here for about two minutes.
Please do not exit the train.
KOFF!
HERE, MISTER!
!

THIS IS FOR YOU.
......
WHY THANK YOU!
MY NAME IS WAKA-CHAN.
WHAT'S YOUR NAME, MISTER?
SEIYA.
MY NAME IS SEIYA.
!
?

KYAAA
AAA
AAAAAAH!
A DREAM?!
PANT!
PANT!
OR IS THIS WHAT I HAVE BEEN TRYING TO FORGET?

WA
A
A
A
AH!

NOOO!

AAAAAARGH!
HOT...
SOMEBODY...
SOMEBODY, GIVE ME WATER...
I CAN'T BREATHE.
HELP...
OH, GOD...
IT'S HAPPENING AGAIN...
GYAAAA
AA
HELP... ME...
AAAAAA
AAH!
S-SEIYA...

QUICK! PUSH THE ALARM!
THAT VOICE?!
WH- WHO?!
HURRY UP! IF YOU'RE CAUGHT, YOU WON'T SURVIVE!
AAHH...
oooH...
ALARM?!
!
Emergency Alarm
Alarm

AAAAH!
HELP!
?!

WHOA!
AH!
AAAAH!
AAH!
!

SE--
SEIYA-SAN?
!

IT'S ME! WAKANA!
THIS GIRL IS...
MY NAME IS WAKA-CHAN.
...FROM THAT DAY...
WHAT'S YOUR NAME, MISTER?
SEIYA.
MY NAME IS SEIYA.
?!
WHAT?!

I WANT TO DIE. DEATH. DEATH!! I'LL KILL ALL OF THEM!! EVERY LAST ONE!!
A POWERFUL EVIL...
I DON'T WANT TO DIE ALONE! DEATH. DIE.
NOT GOOD!!

AAAH!!
WHAT'S HAPPENING?!
AHH...
UGHH...
AHH...
AHH...
FIRE!
RUN!
NOW!
BURNING...
HELP ME...
ARRGHHH!!
AAAH!
MOVE IT!
GET OUT!
C'MON. YOU'VE GOT TO GO!
WAIT, MY DAUGHTER IS STILL INSIDE!

WAAAH
YOU CAN'T!
IT'S TOO LATE!
WAKANA!
WAKANA!
THAT GIRL IS STILL...
HER FLAME OF LIFE IS...
HEY, IT'S TOO DANGER-OUS!
COME BACK!

HUFF!
HUFF!
MOMMY, HELP!
I'M SCARED!!
M-MISTER?

HELP! GRAB HER, QUICK!
MISTER!!
MISTER!!
MISTER !!
MISTER SEIYA!
MISTER!
SEIYA...!
......
SEIYA...

MMM...?
......
WHERE AM I...?
THE UNDER-WORLD.
?!
THE REALM WHERE THOSE WHO ARE FINISHED ON EARTH GATHER FOR ETERNITY.
THE UNDER-WORLD.
UNDER-WORLD? AM I DEAD...?

IS THIS BECAUSE I COULDN'T SAVE THEM?
BUT THERE WAS NOTHING I COULD DO!
EVEN IN DEATH, YOU HAVE REGRETS?
I CAN SEE THEIR FLAMES, BUT THAT'S ALL. I CAN'T SAVE THEM!
I... I...!
YOU HAVE A GIFT, BUT YOU CURSE ITS USELESSNESS. PERHAPS YOU ARE WORTHY...
...OF A LITTLE MORE POWER.
YOU WILL BE ABLE TO CHOOSE WHO SHOULD LIVE...
...AND LEAD THEM TO THE CORRECT PATH.

I HAVE GRANTED YOU THIS POWER. YOU MUST CHOOSE HOW YOU WILL USE IT.
SEIYA, DETERMINE YOUR OWN DESTINY.
SEIYA.
SEIYA...
YOU'RE SEIYA-SAN, AREN'T YOU?!
!
UN-BELIEV-ABLE...
SHE SURVIVED...
I WANTED TO SEE YOU AGAIN.
WHEN I FIRST SAW YOU, I COULD TELL--
YOU SHOULD STOP LOOKING FOR ME.
HOW COULD I? I HAD TO SEE YOU!
!

REMEMBERING SUCH AN EVIL DAY...
...WILL ONLY HURT YOU.
UM... ERR... EXCUSE ME.
HM?
I'D LIKE TO TAKE MY PHOTO HERE.
HUH?!
OH... I-I'M SORRY!
AND THEN I REALIZED...

WAKANA, WHAT WERE YOU DOING THERE?
...I WAS SLEEPING IN THE PHOTO BOOTH.
IT'S WEIRD. I CAN'T REMEMBER ANYTHING.
ザァァ
COME ON. GIVE ME A BREAK!
HA HA HA!!
DARK METRO VOLUME 1...END

POSTSCRIPT

WRITER: TOKYO CALEN

HELLO, EVERYONE! IT'S BEEN ONE YEAR SINCE MY DREAM WAS FIRST REALIZED. AND IT'S THANKS TO YOU ALL THAT THIS BOOK CAME OUT. WHILE WRITING THE STORIES FOR *DARK METRO* AT NIGHT, I'D OFTEN SENSE BEINGS STANDING RIGHT BEHIND MY BACK. AND WHILE WALKING UNDERGROUND IN SUBWAY HALLS, I'D SEE SMALL CRACKS WIDEN. IT HAPPENED WAY TOO MUCH FOR MY OWN GOOD. HA HA HA... ANYWAY, I'LL KEEP TRYING MY BEST, SO THANK YOU FOR YOUR SUPPORT!

◆TOKYO CALEN◆

BORN AND RAISED IN TOKYO. LEO. SPLIT-PERSONALITY OF THE AB BLOOD TYPE.

RECEIVED NUMEROUS AWARDS FOR WRITING FOR MOVIES AND TELEVISION DRAMAS. ALSO WORKS AS A DIRECTOR FOR SHORT FILMS, AND HAS EXPERIENCE WRITING SCRIPTS FOR AND EDITING RADIO DRAMAS. (WILL DO ALMOST ANY TYPE OF WORK.)

HOBBIES INCLUDE...WELL, I WANT TO SAY "WORK," ^_^ BUT LET'S SETTLE WITH WATCHING MOVIES, APPRECIATING MODERN ART, TRAVELING, ETC. I REALLY LOVE TAKING A WALK OUTSIDE TO ESCAPE REALITY.

LIKES: THE OCEAN (MY GRANDPA SAYS OUR ANCESTORS WERE PIRATES), HIGH PLACES, DRIED FRUITS, DRINKING, AND FORTUNE TELLING.

DISLIKES: STICKY AND DISGUSTING BUGS.

HAS A DUEL PERSONALITY OF "LIGHT AND NATURAL" AND "COOL AND OBSERVANT." I CONSIDER MYSELF AN OBEDIENT CITIZEN, BUT PEOPLE OFTEN TELL ME THAT I'M LIKE THE BOSS PULLING STRINGS FROM THE SHADOWS. ^_^;

ARTIST: YOSHIKEN

NICE TO MEET YOU. MY NAME IS YOSHIKEN, AND I WAS THE ARTIST FOR THIS STORY. I RECEIVED A LOT OF HELP FROM A LOT OF PEOPLE TO MAKE THIS VOLUME COME OUT, AND I THANK THEM ALL SINCERELY FOR THAT. TO BE HONEST, I'M PRETTY MUCH A SCAREDY-CAT AT HEART, SO WHILE I WAS DRAWING, I MADE SURE TO PUT IN A LOT OF MY NERVOUSNESS AND FEAR INTO THE PRODUCT. I KNOW THERE'S STILL A LOT I'M NOT GOOD AT, BUT I'VE BEEN IMPROVING WITH EACH PASSING DAY, AND I HOPE THAT YOU STICK WITH US FOR FUTURE VOLUMES.

◆YOSHIKEN◆

A HERMIT LIVING IN YOKOHAMA AREA. SOURCES OF ENERGY: COFFEE AND CIGARETTES. FRIENDS CLAIM HIS AURA HAS TURNED BLACKER SINCE WORKING ON THIS MANGA.

AFTER GRADUATING FROM MULTI-MEDIA ART ACADEMY VOCATIONAL SCHOOL, HE SPENT HIS DAYS WORKING PART-TIME AS AN ASSISTANT. VARIOUS CIRCUMSTANCES LED TO HIM RECEIVING THIS JOB OF DRAWING HORROR MANGA.

LOVES LOUNGING AROUND BY HIMSELF, AND THE MINOR LEAGUES. LOVES HIS XBOX 360 AND HIS CAT.

HATES LONG NIGHTS OF WORK, CROWDED PLACES, AND HIMSELF.

SCARED OF ONIONS AND BIG DOGS. STILL SUCKS AT USING TONE PROGRAMS.

ドク
RIK--
ドクン
TONIGHT-- THE NIGHT A NEW MOON IS BORN.
THE FIRST HARMONY... IS SET.

Find out what happens in *Doors of Chaos* volume 1.
Coming out February 2008!

MORE HORROR AWAITS IN THE NEXT VOLUME OF...

DARK METRO

TERROR AWAITS THE CAREFREE YOUTH OF TOKYO, WITH GRUESOME LESSONS ONLY THE DEAD CAN TEACH. AND THE SOLEMN GUIDE SEIYA FINALLY REVEALS HIS OWN DARK PAST.

Now for a sneak preview of

Four doors exist in this world, protecting it from the demon realm.

Open those doors, and you unleash chaos into the world...

Hear me, o laws that govern this body.
I hereby mend the wounded Harmonies within you.
Damaged nature, be thee righted. Disrupted order, be thee corrected.
O Harmonies that define and bind this life...

...be thee returned to thy proper flow...
WHOOSH
PE-PEEP
PEEP
OH...
OH, MY GOD!! I DID IT! I DID IT! I FINALLY DID IT!!
I FINALLY MANAGED TO FIX THE MUDDLED HARMONY IN A WOUNDED ANIMAL!
"HARMONIES"...
THEY ARE THE LAWS OF NATURE THAT FORM AND CONTROL THE ENTIRE WORLD.
WITHOUT THEM, NOTHING COULD EXIST.
GOD, WOULD YOU BE STILL?
PROPER HARMONIZERS DO NOT GO BOUNCING OFF THE WALLS IN JOY EVERY TIME THEY MANAGE TO DO THEIR JOB CORRECTLY.

HOWEVER, IT IS GOOD TO KNOW YOU HAVE MASTERED ALL THE STAGES BEFORE YOUR COMING OF AGE CEREMONY.
WELL DONE, MIZERIA.
RIKHTER!
HOW CAN YOU BE SO COLD? YOU'RE MY TUTOR! TUTORS ARE SUPPOSED TO BE HAPPY WHEN THEIR STUDENTS SUCCEED!
MIZERIA, CONGRATULATIONS!
EEP!

OOH, I'M SO HAPPY! NOW WE WON'T HAVE ANYTHING TO WORRY ABOUT GOING INTO OUR 16TH BIRTHDAY TWO DAYS FROM NOW! ♡
EVER SINCE WE WERE LITTLE, YOU WERE ALWAYS SLOW TO LEARN AND GOT CONFUSED BY THE SIMPLEST THINGS...
...BUT NOW YOU'VE FINALLY LEARNED SO MUCH THAT YOU'RE ALMOST IN THE SAME LEAGUE AS RIKHTER AND I! ISN'T THAT WONDERFUL?
C--
CLARISSA...!
CLARISSA. THAT WAS HARDLY A COMPLIMENT.
IT WASN'T?
I HAVE WATCHED OVER YOU TWO FOR MANY LONG YEARS. I CAN ATTEST TO HOW WELL YOU HAVE GROWN. BOTH OF YOU HAVE BECOME MATURE, RESPECTABLE YOUNG LADIES.
Almost in the same league...
DO NOT BE TROUBLED, MIZERIA.
IS THAT NOT ENOUGH?
...
I'M NOT A CHILD ANY MORE, SO YOU DON'T HAVE TO TREAT ME LIKE ONE, OKAY?

I'M NOT GOING TO NEED YOU AROUND TO LEAN ON FOREVER, YOU KNOW!
MY YOUNGER TWIN SISTER, CLARISSA, AND I...
...WERE BORN AND RAISED IN THE LOCKED GARDEN, IN THE HEART OF THE ROYAL PALACE OF THE KINGDOM OF DRUADDLE.
WE WERE TOLD OUR PARENTS DIED SOON AFTER WE WERE BORN. RIKHTER HAS BEEN COMING HERE AS OUR TUTOR FOR AS LONG AS WE REMEMBER.
HARDLY A DAY GOES BY THAT THE THREE OF US DON'T SPEND TOGETHER--
...NH!
UGH...!
MIZERIA?!

RIKHTER, HURRY!
SHE'S HAVING ANOTHER ONE OF HER ATTACKS!
HAHN...
HNN...
NGK!
LET ME SEE.
Hff!
Hah!
MIZERIA, CAN YOU HEAR ME? MIZERIA?
Hff!
Hff!
UH-OH... NOT GOOD.
MY VISION'S... FADING...
DARN IT... NOT AGAIN...!
CAN'T... HOLD ON...TO CONSCIOUSNESS...

"HARMONIZER"?
YES.
THE WORLD EXISTS AS IT IS BECAUSE ALL THE HARMONIES ARE IN BALANCE.
AND EVERYTHING IN THE WORLD, INCLUDING YOU AND ME, HAS A HARMONY.
NOW, SOME PEOPLE ARE BORN WITH THE ABILITY TO CORRECT THE DISRUPTIONS THAT OCCASIONALLY HAPPEN TO A HARMONY.
THOSE PEOPLE ARE CALLED HARMONIZERS.
OH...
SO WHAT'S THAT GOT TO DO WITH US?
EVERYTHING.
YOU SEE, ALL HARMONIZERS MUST BE BROUGHT TO AND RAISED IN THE PALACE.

AND YOU, MIZERIA, CLARISSA...
...ARE TWO OF THE VERY FEW PEOPLE IN THE WORLD WHO CAN BECOME HARMONIZERS.
Huff...
RIK...
THERE.
MUCH BET-TER.
MIZERIA, ARE YOU ALL RIGHT?
ARE YOU SURE YOU DIDN'T PUSH YOURSELF TOO HARD IN YOUR TRAINING FOR THE COMING OF AGE CEREMONY?
SHE HAS A POINT. IF YOU OVERWORK YOURSELF, THE CEREMONY WILL BE THE LEAST OF YOUR WORRIES.

N-NO! I'M FINE!
I'M FINE, I SWEAR! IN FACT, I'VE BEEN FEELING BETTER THAN USUAL LATELY! I--
Uph!
YOU WILL STAY LYING DOWN UNTIL I SAY OTHERWISE.
HIS LONG, WARM FINGERS ALWAYS SOOTHE AWAY ALL MY WORRIES...
...AND GENTLY GATHER MY SCATTERED THOUGHTS AND FEELINGS.
EVER SINCE I WAS LITTLE...
...I'VE BEEN WEAK AND SICKLY. THOUGH I'VE LOST COUNT OF THE NUMBER OF TIMES I'VE BEEN BEDRIDDEN, I KNOW THAT EVERY TIME, JUST THE TOUCH OF RIKHTER'S HAND WAS ENOUGH TO MAKE ME FEEL WORLDS BETTER.
THOUGH YOU ALWAYS DID HAVE PROBLEMS SLEEPING WITHOUT ME NEARBY, DIDN'T YOU?
!!
Chuckle
DO YOU NEED ME TO LIE NEXT TO YOU AND CODDLE YOU TO SLEEP AGAIN TODAY?

OH? ARE YOU ABSOLUTELY SURE YOU'LL BE OKAY?
N-N-NO! THAT WAS AGES AGO!!
I'M NOT A LITTLE KID ANYMORE! I CAN GET TO SLEEP JUST FINE ON MY OWN! AND YOU DON'T HAVE TO KEEP STANDING OVER ME, EITHER!
YES! I'LL BE FINE, CLARISSA! NOW, YOU SHOULD PRACTICE YOUR HARMONIZING FOR RIKHTER INSTEAD OF DALLYING AROUND HERE.
'KAY?
HAVE FUN!
....
THAT'S RIGHT.
I'M...
...NOT A LITTLE KID ANY MORE.
HARMONIZING IS A DANGEROUS SKILL. USE IT INCORRECTLY, AND YOU COULD WIND UP DESTROYING YOURSELF.
CLARISSA AND I WERE BROUGHT TO THE LOCKED GARDEN SO THAT WE COULD LEARN THE CORRECT WAY TO USE OUR POWER.

YEAH...
I'VE ALWAYS WANTED TO SEE THE OUTSIDE. AND AFTER THE CEREMONY, THEY'LL LET ME DO THAT.
THAT'S GREAT. REALLY. IT IS. BUT...
BUT I CAN'T HELP BUT FEEL LIKE SOMETHING... ISN'T RIGHT.
MAYBE I'M AFRAID BECAUSE, FROM WHAT I'VE HEARD, THE OUTSIDE IS A TERRIFYINGLY HUGE PLACE.
OR MAYBE I'M JUST WORRIED BECAUSE, AFTER WE LEAVE THE LOCKED GARDEN, I MIGHT NOT BE ABLE TO SPEND EVERY DAY WITH CLARISSA AND RIKHTER ANYMORE.
I JUST CAN'T QUITE PUT MY FINGER ON WHAT IT IS.

I FEEL LIKE I SHOULD KNOW WHAT IT IS, BUT I DON'T. STRANGE...
OUT FOR A WALK BY YOURSELF AT THIS HOUR? HOW TERRIBLY UNUSUAL.
AND AREN'T YOU GOING IN THE WRONG DIRECTION? THE LOCKED GARDEN, WHERE YOUR PRECIOUS PRINCESSES SLEEP, LAYS THE OTHER WAY.
IT IS HARDLY COMMON FOR YOU TO BE FOUND ALL THE WAY OVER HERE YOURSELF, SIR.
DO YOU HAVE BUSINESS WITH ME?
NO, NO. I JUST WANTED TO SEE YOU.
OH, YOUR PRINCESSES WILL BE ADULTS THIS COMING EVE.
YOU MUST BE SO TERRIBLY... PROUD...
TA-TA...
Hee hee hee...

......
THIS WILL BE THE 16TH TIME CLARISSA AND I HAVE CELEBRATED OUR BIRTHDAY.
WE'VE PREPARED FOR OUR COMING OF AGE CEREMONY FOR A LONG TIME...BUT, HONESTLY, I DON'T KNOW WHAT IT WILL INVOLVE.
AFTER ALL...A SICK, WEAK CHILD IS ALL I EVER WAS.

OH...
...WOW!!
THE DAY OF THE CEREMONY.
SO...
SO THIS IS THE DRUADDLE ROYAL PALACE!
OH, MY GOD! I'M SO NERVOUS, I FEEL LIKE I MIGHT FAINT!
MY LADY, THE CEREMONY WILL SOON BEGIN. IF YOU WOULD PLEASE MAKE YOUR WAY TO THE GREAT HALL...
O-OH! OF COURSE! I-I'M SORRY!
AND I HAVEN'T BEEN ABLE TO SEE CLARISSA OR RIKHTER SINCE THIS MORNING, EITHER!

コッ
HERE WE GO... MY FIRST STEPS OUTSIDE...
コッ
コッ
ICK.
I CAN FEEL EVERYBODY STARING AT ME. IT'S GIVING ME THE CREEPS...
OH.
THERE'S CLARISSA!
Whew!
EVERYTHING WILL BE ALL RIGHT.

I'LL BE FINE. I'VE GOT THE RITUAL EXPRESSION OF GRATITUDE AND HARMONIZERS' ACKNOWLEDGEMENT OF DUTIES SPEECHES DOWN COLD.
I, MIZERIA REZELPUT, SPEAKING ON BEHALF OF MYSELF AND MY SISTER, CLARISSA REZELPUT...
...DO HEREBY EXTEND OUR ETERNAL GRATITUDE FOR THE MOST GENEROUS CARE AND PROTECTION AFFORDED TO US...
...BY HIS MAJESTY, KING REICHNET ADEUALA DRUADDLE.
THERE! I SAID IT PERFECTLY!
STAYING UP ALL LAST NIGHT MEMORIZING IT PAID OFF!
NEXT IS THE HARMONIZERS' ACKNOWLEDGEMENT OF DUTIES.
IT IS THANKS ENTIRELY TO HIS MAJESTY'S KINDNESS AND CARE THAT WE ARE HERE TODAY.
IF I CAN JUST PULL THAT ONE OFF, THEN...

...AH!
?!
...AAAAAAAH!!!
WHAT THE--?!
WHAT'S GOING ON?!
MY BODY! IT FEELS LIKE...I'M ON FIRE!

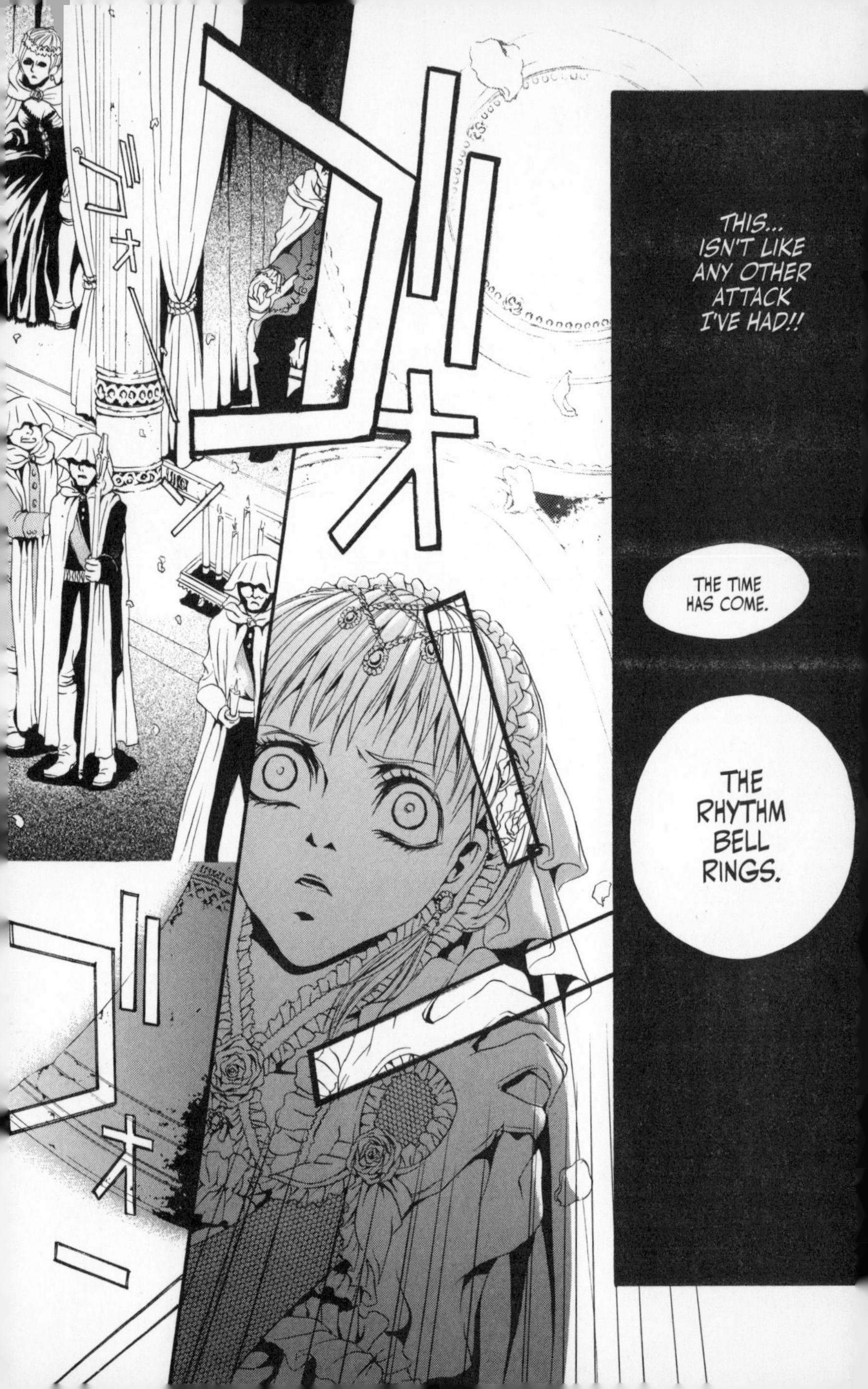
THIS... ISN'T LIKE ANY OTHER ATTACK I'VE HAD!!
THE TIME HAS COME.
THE RHYTHM BELL RINGS.

WHA...?
WHERE'S THE SOUND OF THAT BELL COMING FROM?!
OOH!
THIS DIURNAL LADY LOOKS JUST LIKE THE OTHER ONE!
BUT SHE HAS BLACK HAIR INSTEAD OF BLOND.
WHICH MEANS...
...YOU MUST BE MIZERIA, THE LIVING KEY!

YEEK!
I'M SO HONORED TO MEET YOU, MISS!
MY NAME IS LUCIANO. I'M ALSO CALLED "THE CRIMSON SHADOW." ♡
OH, MY GOD!
WHERE DID THIS GIRL COME FROM?! SHE JUST...WALKED OUT OF THIN AIR!
EANEY!
NELEURO!
I FOUND THE LIVING KEY FIRST! I WIN! ♡
SCLORP
!!
KYAAAH!

OH, DEAR. OH, DEAR.
IT SEEMS YOU HAVE QUITE GOTTEN THE BETTER OF ME, LADY LUCIANO.
BECOMING LOST IN THE ENDLESS HALLS OF THIS PALACE WAS A GRAVE FAILING ON MY PART INDEED.
GOOD TO MEET YOU, SIRS, MADAMS. I AM EANEY, THE "SMILING MAN."
TO MY RIGHT IS OUR COMPANION, NELEURO, ALSO CALLED "OLD MAN CARRION."
WHAT'S THIS?!
N-NO...
IT CAN'T BE...!
THEY'RE... THEY'RE...
EVERYONE AT FULL ATTENTION!!
KILL THOSE MONSTERS AT ONCE!

CLARISSA!
I HAVE NO IDEA WHAT'S GOING ON, BUT IT LOOKS REALLY BAD!
LET'S FIND RIKHTER AND RU--
CL... CLARI...
...SSA...?
WHA...?
WHY...?

KYAAAA!!
LADY HAINA!
MADAM!
LORD NORTON? LORD NORTON! SAY SOMETHING!
LORD KLAUF!!
GOOD GODS! SOMETHING'S KILLING MEMBERS OF THE ROYAL FAMILY!!
WHAT HAPPENED TO THE GUARDS?! WHY HAVEN'T THEY DONE ANYTHING?!
TH-THE GUARDS ARE ALL DEAD!!
OH, MY GOD... OH, MY GOD...
WHAT'S HAPPENING?! WHAT'S GOING ON?!

わ
W
あ
A
A
A
あ
A
A
あ
A
A
あ
あ
A!
......
WHERE... WHERE ARE THEY?
WHERE ARE CLARISSA AND RIKHTER...?
THIS...
THIS CAN'T ALL BE PART OF THE COMING OF AGE CEREMONY...
...CAN IT?
W-WHY IS ALL THIS HAPPENING...?
IF...
IF ANYTHING'S HAPPENED TO CLARISSA AND RIKHTER, I... I--!!
COME, COME, MILADY LIVING KEY.
YOU NEED NOT FEAR FOR THAT GENTLEMAN AND HIS LADY.
FOR EVEN AT THIS VERY MOMENT...

...THEY ARE STANDING DIRECTLY BEHIND YOU.
RIKHTER...?
CLARISSA...?

RIK--
TONIGHT-- THE NIGHT A NEW MOON IS BORN.
THE FIRST HARMONY... IS SET.

Find out what happens in *Doors of Chaos* volume 1. Coming out February 2008!

STOP!

This is the back of the book.
You wouldn't want to spoil a great ending!

This book is printed "manga-style," in the authentic Japanese right-to-left format. Since none of the artwork has been flipped or altered, readers get to experience the story just as the creator intended. You've been asking for it, so TOKYOPOP® delivered: authentic, hot-off-the-press, and far more fun!

DIRECTIONS

If this is your first time reading manga-style, here's a quick guide to help you understand how it works.

It's easy... just start in the top right panel and follow the numbers. Have fun, and look for more 100% authentic manga from TOKYOPOP®!